Siamese Cats

by Meredith Dash

ABDO
CATS
Kids

www.abdopublishing.com

Published by Abdo Kids, a division of ABDO, P.O. Box 398166, Minneapolis, Minnesota 55439.

Printed in the United States of America, North Mankato, Minnesota.

052014

092014

 THIS BOOK CONTAINS
RECYCLED MATERIALS

Photo Credits: iStock, Shutterstock, Thinkstock

Production Contributors: Teddy Borth, Jennie Forsberg, Grace Hansen

Design Contributors: Candice Keimig, Laura Rask, Dorothy Toth

Library of Congress Control Number: 2013952416

Cataloging-in-Publication Data

Dash, Meredith.

 Siamese cats / Meredith Dash.

  p. cm. -- (Cats)

ISBN 978-1-62970-013-7 (lib. bdg.)

Includes bibliographical references and index.

1. Siamese cats--Juvenile literature.   I. Title.

636.8--dc23

                    2013952416

Table of Contents

Siamese Cats

Siamese cats are one of the most popular **breeds**. They are loving and **loyal** cats.

Siamese cats have beautiful

blue eyes. They have very

large ears.

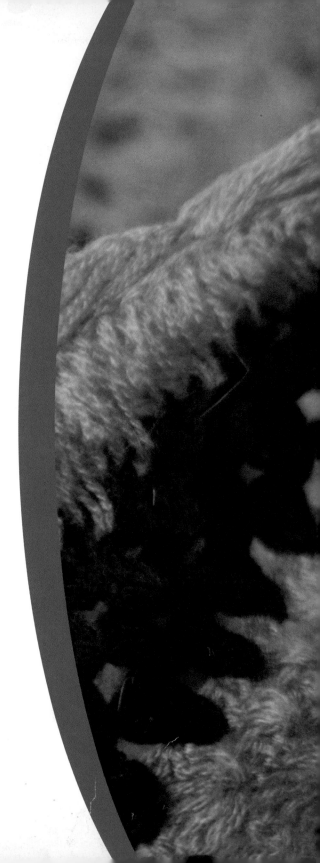

Siamese cats have short coats.

Their coats are a cream color.

A Siamese cat's face and paws

are brown. Its tail is brown too.

11

Siamese cats have long tails.

Some have a **kink** in their tails.

13

Smart Cats

Siamese cats are smart. It is easy to teach them new tricks.

Personality

Siamese cats are known for their deep meow. They meow when they need something.

17

Siamese cats are social.

They are happy to play

or be near you.

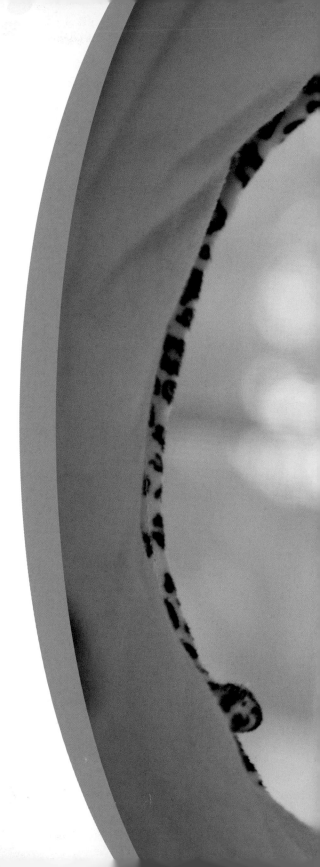

Siamese cats are good with children and other animals. But they will be especially **loyal** to one person.

More Facts

- Siamese cats are one of the oldest **breeds** of cat. They are thought to have originated from Thailand. Thailand used to be called Siam.

- Siamese cats tend to be jealous. They would not be happy if you brought home another animal.

- You can teach a Siamese cat to play fetch!

Glossary

breed – a group of animals sharing
the same looks and features.

kink – a small twist, bend, or curl.

loyal – faithful or devoted to someone
or something.

social – friendly, enjoys being around others.

Index

abdokids.com

Use this code to log on to abdokids.com and access crafts, games, videos and more!

Abdo Kids Code:
CSK0137